the little book of
SPELLS

Published by OH!
20 Mortimer Street
London W1T 3JW

Disclaimer:
This book and the information contained herein are for general educational and entertainment use only. The contents are not claimed to be exhaustive, and the book is sold on the understanding that neither the publishers nor the author are thereby engaged in rendering any kind of professional services. Users are encouraged to confirm the information contained herein with other sources and review the information carefully with their appropriate, qualified service providers. Neither the publishers nor the author shall have any responsibility to any person or entity regarding any loss or damage whatsoever, direct or indirect, consequential, special or exemplary, caused or alleged to be caused, by the use or misuse of information contained in this book.

ISBN 978-1-91161-076-2

Editorial consultant: Sasha Fenton
Editorial: Jacqueline Towers, Victoria Godden
Project managers: Russell Porter
Design: Ben Ruocco
Production: Rachel Burgess

A CIP catalogue record for this book is available from the British Library

Printed in China

10 9 8 7 6 5 4

the little book of
SPELLS

jacqueline towers

CONTENTS

INTRODUCTION

A spell, also known as an incantation, can be a way of producing a positive effect either in the life of the caster or those of others. Spells can consist of a ritual action, usually through a set of words or a verse or any combination of these. While some spells may require certain ingredients and ritualistic actions, other spells only require a recitation, all of which you will find within this book.

It is always advisable to work with the Archangels for the sake of safety and also to achieve the right effect from your spells, so always ask for protection from one of these Archangels before setting out to cast any kind of spell.

To do this, relax in a quiet place and allow yourself to drift into a kind of half-asleep trance, and then ask your Archangel to give you the protection you need and also to protect those for whom you may be spellcasting.

The four primary Archangels are: Michael, Gabriel, Raphael and Uriel. Their characteristics are as follows:

michael Protection, truth, integrity, strength and courage

gabriel Communication skills, purity, harmony and creativity

raphael Healing and travel

uriel Solving problems and resolving conflicts, wisdom, emotional imbalance and determination

top ten
TIPS

never cast spells for ill-will against anybody

never cast spells to alter someone's own free will

never cast a spell to make someone fall in love with you

never cast a spell on or for someone without their permission

never restart a spell once you have started

always protect yourself before conducting a spell

always work with the Archangels

always use new candles and incense sticks

always end your chant with the words "so mote it be". If you want the spell to be stronger, repeat these words three times

always close your chakras down after casting a spell. You will see how to do this later in this book

CHAPTER

1

TOOLS
you will need

You will need the following:

a cloth – which can be any colour

a pentagram – make this by drawing the symbol in white or silver onto a piece of black card about the size of a small dinner plate, and then cut the card into a circle. This will serve as your main focal point, but the following items should be placed around the pentagram in the stated positions:

west – A glass or cup of water. This will represent the emotions and flexibility

north – Stones, crystal or salt to represent the earth and anything practical

east – Incense to represent air, indicating reflection and communication

south – A candle, representing fire, characterising inspiration and action

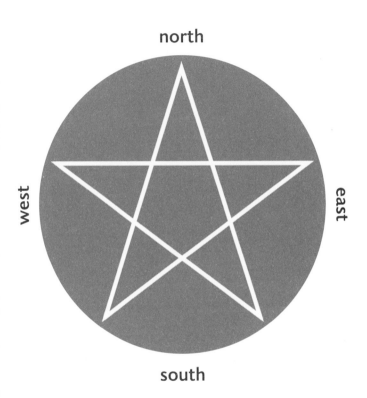

north

west

east

south

making an
ALTAR

Find a quiet place in which to make your altar
and then place your cloth on it. Put your
pentagram in the middle of the cloth together
with your elements of air, water, earth and fire
in their correct positions.

You need to cleanse your space before
you start casting spells. You can do this by
imagining a pure white light from above your
head coming down and enveloping you and
your altar. Alternatively, you can cleanse your
area by lighting a sage stick and waving it over
your altar.

Charge your pentagram by placing both hands upon it and state out loud that you want it and the items placed around it to work with you and the Archangels. Do not rush this! It is important that you feel the change in the energy.

Do not worry if you appear to feel very hot during this process. It is perfectly normal and is a positive sign that you have connected with your pentagram.

Call in the Archangel you wish to work with and when you have completed your spellcasting, always thank the Angel who has worked with you.

Warning: Be extremely careful what you spell for, because when spellcasting, it goes out three-fold, but it can also come back three-fold.

CHAPTER

2

SPELLS

for

BEGINNERS

Have confidence in the spell, believe it will come true and use a spell written as a poem or a chant to help increase the power of the spell. Meditation prior to spellcasting will help to connect you to your pentagram and those you wish to call upon, as it is necessary to use strong concentration and to focus with intent. This will project your spell and give it more power. Be patient and make sure you give the spell time to work.

PROTECTION
spell

I call upon the four elements from
the four corners of the Earth to protect me
in this hour of need.
Earth, air, fire and water, please protect me now.
So mote it be.

GOOD LUCK
spell

Good luck is what I want. Good luck is what
I need. I call upon Archangel Michael to
complete this deed.
When I finish reciting this spell, all bad luck
will be dispensed with.
So mote it be.

MONEY

I call upon Archangel Gabriel to bring to
me prosperity and do away with austerity.
So mote it be.

HEALTH

I call upon Archangel Raphael to
bring health to both my body and mind
and to make me stronger.
Please make it so.
So mote it be.

CHANGE of LUCK

I call upon Archangel Michael to change
my luck this night.
Together with the help from all the stars so bright.
So mote it be.

LOVE

I call upon Archangel Michael to find me a lover
and one that will last.
This is what I spell for, and so it is cast.
So mote it be.

helping someone recover from
ILLNESS

I call upon Archangel Uriel by the sun
and by the moon,

I ask that you make _____ well again

very soon.

So mote it be.

ANXIETY

I call upon Archangel Michael to remove all my
worries and my fears,
So I no longer have the need to shed any more tears.
Bring peace into my life now and show me the way,
To happier times and a brighter day.
So mote it be.

ILLNESS

I call upon Archangel Raphael
to remove my illness and return my health,
And bring me back to my healthy self.
So mote it be.

CHAPTER

3

CANDLE COLOURS,
astrology and
days of the week

This chapter shows you how to choose the
right coloured candle and the right day of
the week for your spell. It also explains the
magical, astrological significance that is linked
to each spell.

RED
ARIES
TUESDAY

- Symbolizes everything to do with sexuality, love and marriage
- Has a positive effect on courage and willpower as well as fertility
- Can increase magnetism, faith, vitality, communication and protection

ORANGE
LEO
SUNDAY

- Symbolizes transformation, energy, luck, adaptability
- Can help with attractiveness and weight loss
- Good for dealing with authority, legal cases and justice, also anything to do with trade, property and business

PINK
TAURUS
FRIDAY

- Symbolizes honesty, reputation and respect
- Can increase affection, love, amicability, faithfulness, femininity and charm
- Brings understanding, clarity, prediction, education and reconciliation

PURPLE

SCORPIO
TUESDAY

- Inspiration, business development, competence, dominance, success
- Good for understanding, hidden knowledge, opening the third eye, meditation, improving psychic abilities
- Helps with difficult illnesses

LAVENDER
VIRGO
WEDNESDAY

- Help with getting a tough job done
- Creative ideas and problem solving
- Improvement in health for self and family members

YELLOW
GEMINI
WEDNESDAY

- Brings self-confidence in spellcasting, setting intention and successful rituals
- Symbolizes energy, creativity, charisma, intelligence, improvement in memory and wisdom
- Eliminates blocks and obstacles

BROWN

CAPRICORN

SATURDAY

- Good for healing, animal spellcraft, connection to animals, animal cures
- Symbolizes earthly bonds, consistency, education, intuition
- Can help with finding lost objects and professional affairs

BLUE
PISCES
THURSDAY

- Symbolizes wisdom, harmony, intuition, peace, truth, luck, protection
- Can provide spiritual inspiration and prophetic dreams

GOLD
LEO
SUNDAY

- Add some fun to a life that is flat and boring
- Success with parties, social life and romantic meetings
- Success with tests, exams and interviews

DARK BLUE
AQUARIUS
SATURDAY

- Removes despair, despondency, impulsiveness or vulnerability
- When fresh ideas are needed
- Adds a touch of originality and fun

INDIGO
SAGITTARIUS
THURSDAY

- Brings luck with travel and new enterprises
- Can help when you need to go into a deep meditation

GREEN
LIBRA
FRIDAY

- Symbolizes wealth, fertility, success
- Good for finances, luck, money, career, accomplishment of personal goals, job placement
- Can increase determination and willpower
- Helps to restore youth and beauty

EMERALD GREEN

TAURUS
FRIDAY

- Symbolizes enchanting love, social pleasures, fertility
- Helps get rid of illness, cowardliness, indignation, resentment, jealousy, disagreements

DARK GREEN
CAPRICORN
SATURDAY

- Clears opposition, blocks to ambition and initiative
- Helps cope with those who are resentful, jealous and unpleasant

SILVER
CANCER
MONDAY

- Removes negative energy, supports dependability
- Helps develop spiritual energy, psychic powers, intuition and dreams
- Enhances shrewdness, recovery from loss and growth

GREY

CAPRICORN
SATURDAY

- Symbolizes magnetism, attractiveness
- Make difficult tasks easier to do
- Can cancel things that are no longer needed
- Good for meditation and reflection

BLACK
SCORPIO
TUESDAY

- Eliminates evil spirits, absorbs and destroys negative energy, removes obstacles
- Used for deep states of meditation and psychic development

WHITE

CANCER
MONDAY

- Symbolizes purity, truth, integrity, wisdom
- Used for spiritual enlightenment and forgiveness
- Can help with matters of prophecy, healing, peace, virtuousness, divinity and security
- Balances all other colours and can replace any of the other colours if required

CHAPTER

4

STAR SIGNS, LUCKY DAYS and COLOURS

Certain days are lucky for certain signs of the zodiac. Also, particular colours have magical associations with the signs, so you might want to use a candle of a particular colour or perhaps write your spell on a piece of coloured paper. As you will see, some colours can be used together in a combination, for instance two candles or a candle in one colour and some paper in another.

ARIES

(March, 21 – April, 19)

day: Tuesday
colour: Red, white/pink, white/red

TAURUS

(April, 20 – May, 20)

day: Friday
colour: Pink, green/brown, pink/green

GEMINI

(May, 21 – June, 21)

day: Wednesday
colour: Yellow, yellow/dark blue,
red/dark blue

CANCER

(June, 22 – July, 22)

day: Monday
colour: Dark green, light blue/white,
white/brown

LEO

(July, 23 – August, 22)

day: Sunday
colour: Orange, orange/red, red/green

VIRGO

(August, 23 – September, 22)

day: Wednesday
colour: Blue, yellow/black, yellow/green

LIBRA

(September, 23 – October, 22)

day: Friday
colour: Light blue/pink, blue/black

SCORPIO

(October, 23 – November, 21)

day: Tuesday
colour: Burgundy, red/black,
brown/black

SAGITTARIUS

(November, 22 – December, 21)

day: Thursday
colour: Purple, light blue/purple,
white/purple

CAPRICORN

(December, 22 – January, 19)

day: Saturday
colour: Brown, red/purple, red/brown

AQUARIUS

(January, 20 – February, 18)

day: Saturday
colour: Aqua, blue/green, grey/light
blue

PISCES

(February, 19 – March, 20)

day: Thursday
colour: Light green, white/green,
white/lavender

CHAPTER

5

CANDLES

for HEALING

Either put a photo of the person who needs
healing on your altar or write their name on
a piece of paper and put that on the altar.
Then light candles in the appropriate colour to
activate the healing spell.

RED

for the
head, eyes, skull and upper jaw

PINK

for the
lower jaw, throat (including
the thyroid gland in the neck)
and upper spine

SILVER
or WHITE

for the
lungs, breast, and rib cage; also
the stomach and digestive organs

YELLOW

for the
upper respiratory system, the
brain, shoulders, arms, wrists
and hands

GOLD
or ORANGE

for the

spine, heart, arteries and
circulation

PLUM

for the

bowels, skin and nervous system

LIGHT GREEN

for the
bladder, pancreas and kidneys

MAGENTA

for the
sexual organs in the lower
stomach, lower spine,
reproductive system, blood
and eyes

DARK BLUE

for the
hips, thighs, and the circulation
of blood through the legs

BROWN
or MUSTARD

for the
skin, bones, knees, teeth and
chronic ailments

LIGHT BLUE

for the

ankles, bronchial tubes and skin

TURQUOISE

for the

feet and lungs, but also the mind
and the psychic and intuitive
potential/capability

CHAPTER
6

CANDLE SPELLS

Candle spellcasting is one of the simplest forms of achieving your goal, so you need to choose a sensible, fireproof candle holder that won't fall down, and always use a brand new candle for spell work. Choose the colour of your candle to correspond with what you want to achieve. For instance, for money, you will need a green candle. You can use a tea light candle or one in a container. Light the candle while concentrating on the purpose of the spell, thereby putting the intention into the candle. Call upon the appropriate Archangel to work with you and tell him what it is you want him to help you to achieve.

for creativity –
YELLOW
candle

I call upon Archangel Gabriel,
Stimulation of art, inspiration of sound,
Encouragement of thought gather round.
I summon your power, your guiding light.
Please guide my hand in this creative rite.
And as I call your spirit forth,
So mote it be.

to find a missing or lost item –

BROWN

candle

I call upon Archangel Uriel.

Please give me a peek for what I seek.

I ask that you show me the way,

Of where it may lay.

So mote it be.

overcoming
bereavement –
WHITE
candle

I call upon Archangel Raphael
from all four corners,
Fire, earth and air I release the
spirit of _____
To your eternal care.
So mote it be.

or you can say the following –

I call upon Archangel Raphael to take my
worries, fears and loss,
From my shoulders now.
And bring tranquillity and serenity into my life,
So I can live in peace somehow.
So mote it be.

to find a job –

PURPLE

candle

I call upon Archangel Gabriel with
your great powers and energies to,
Kindly lend a hand, so grateful I will be.
Please help _____ gain a job
that will pay enough,
With plenty to spare, by the power
of three.

So mote it be.

banishing
negative energy –
BLUE
candle

I call upon Archangel Michael
and ask that all,
Negative energy be banished.
Release it and send it on its way.
So mote it be.

seven magical
TIPS

1 Writing your own spells will give them more power and positive results because you are putting your intention into the spell

2 It is advisable to keep a Spell Book or Book of Shadows, as it is sometimes called, to write notes about the spells for future reference

3 You may just write down the appropriate words required for the type of spell you are making, or you can write down the words in rhyme

4 Concentrate on the wording of your spell before you start so that you put your full intention into your spell

5 Never use a candle that has been lit before

6 Snuff the candle out, or if you blow it out, ensure that it goes out and stays out

7 Never leave a burning candle unattended

consider
TIMING

For example, the
times between 9 pm
and midnight are
powerful times

However, when you become more familiar with casting spells, you can see certain days of the week become even more relevant than the time at which you cast the spell. Also, if you happen to be into astrology, you could find the moon's position on any particular day. For example, a full moon in Pisces would be the perfect time to cast a spell to do with creativity.

CHAPTER

7

THE HOUR
and the
PLANET

This well known ancient system links the hours of the day to the planets that are visible to the naked eye. In countries where British Summer Time or Daylight Saving is in operation during part of the year, jump back one hour in the summer months.

HOUR	SUN	MON	TUE
01.00	Sun	Moon	Mars
02.00	Venus	Saturn	Sun
03.00	Mercury	Jupiter	Venus
04.00	Moon	Mars	Mercury
05.00	Saturn	Sun	Moon
06.00	Jupiter	Venus	Saturn
07.00	Mars	Mercury	Jupiter
08.00	Sun	Moon	Mars
09.00	Venus	Saturn	Sun
10.00	Mercury	Jupiter	Venus
11.00	Moon	Mars	Mercury
12.00	Saturn	Sun	Moon
13.00	Jupiter	Venus	Saturn
14.00	Mars	Mercury	Jupiter
15.00	Sun	Moon	Mars
16.00	Venus	Saturn	Sun
17.00	Mercury	Jupiter	Venus
18.00	Moon	Mars	Mercury
19.00	Saturn	Sun	Moon
20.00	Jupiter	Venus	Saturn
21.00	Mars	Mercury	Jupiter
22.00	Sun	Moon	Mars
23.00	Venus	Saturn	Sun
24.00	Mercury	Jupiter	Venus

WED	THU	FRI	SAT
Mercury	Jupiter	Venus	Saturn
Moon	Mars	Mercury	Jupiter
Saturn	Sun	Moon	Mars
Jupiter	Venus	Saturn	Sun
Mars	Mercury	Jupiter	Venus
Sun	Moon	Mars	Mercury
Venus	Saturn	Sun	Moon
Mercury	Jupiter	Venus	Saturn
Moon	Mars	Mercury	Jupiter
Saturn	Sun	Moon	Mars
Jupiter	Venus	Saturn	Sun
Mars	Mercury	Jupiter	Venus
Sun	Moon	Mars	Mercury
Venus	Saturn	Sun	Moon
Mercury	Jupiter	Venus	Saturn
Moon	Mars	Mercury	Jupiter
Saturn	Sun	Moon	Mars
Jupiter	Venus	Saturn	Sun
Mars	Mercury	Jupiter	Venus
Sun	Moon	Mars	Mercury
Venus	Saturn	Sun	Moon
Mercury	Jupiter	Venus	Saturn
Moon	Mars	Mercury	Jupiter
Saturn	Sun	Moon	Mars

the SUN

Solar matters include children, celebrations,
love-making, sports, games and having fun,
business matters, creativity and social life.
The Sun also rules gold and jewellery.

the MOON

Your emotions are likely to be strong during any moon day or hour, especially at the time of a new or full moon, and even more so at the time of an eclipse. Intuition and psychic powers are normally heightened when the moon is prominent. Moon days and hours are particularly good for performing spells that concern home and family.

MERCURY

Mercury rules communications with those who are in your immediate neighbourhood, so for extra power, get your message across on a Wednesday and during a Mercury hour. Mercury is associated with healing, so if a person is suffering from ill health, or even if your friend or loved one is unhappy and sick at heart, a Mercury hour would be a good one to choose for a healing spell.

VENUS

Venus was the Roman goddess of love, so if you are planning a romantic meeting, choose a Venus day or hour for your spell. You can also perform spells for prosperity or abundance during a Venus hour.

MARS

Tackle anything that requires action and activity during a Mars hour.

JUPITER

Jupiter is associated with long-distance travel, business with overseas customers and working with foreigners. It also rules legal matters, education, religion, philosophy and spirituality. Some see Jupiter as a lucky planet that is linked with gambling, especially horse racing.

SATURN

This is a good planet to invoke if you need to bring wisdom to bear on a situation or if you are dealing with older people, father figures or those who are in positions of authority.

an interesting
POINT

There are three months in the year during which it is considered unwise to enter a new house or to sign a lease. These are April, July and November. Neither is the eleventh day of any month good for big projects.

CHAPTER

8

MOON
PHASES

The phases of the moon can be grouped into the new moon, the waxing moon, the full moon and the waning moon. Spells cast at the appropriate time will give them added power, while living by the moon's cycles can help us to feel healthier and more energetic, as well as aiding in supporting us in the release of old habits that no longer serve our highest good.

Note that the new moon looks like the capital letter D, while the really old moon looks like the capital letter C.

the NEW MOON

This is the first phase of the lunar cycle and it begins when you can see a tiny slice of moon.

The new moon represents a fresh start, so it is a good time to set goals and intentions for the approaching cycle.

attributes

- An ideal time to begin any new projects, ask for ideas/inspiration, additional energy, strength and freedom

- An excellent time to cast spells for anything to do with love, financial matters, success, courage, friendship, luck or health

the BLACK MOON

A black, or dark, moon is the name given to the appearance of a second new moon in the same calandar month. This is quite rare, only happening every two to three years, but it is the most favourable time for banishing and neutralizing spells.

The dark moon is a time for dealing with attackers, for exploring our darkest recesses and understanding our angers and passions, also anything to bring justice to bear. It is an extremely potent time for prophecy work.

WAXING MOON

A waxing moon is a moon that is growing from new to full. It is the ideal time for spells for starting new projects, initiation and improvement. "Increase" is the operative word here, because this time of the moon's increasing light is the ideal period to spellcast for anything to do with growth.

the FULL MOON

The days just before the full moon are the most powerful times for success and completion.

attributes

- Spellcasting during a full moon will bring success in achieving goals, development, passion, healing, strength and power

- An excellent time to casr spells related to love, knowledge, any legal undertakings, financial matters and dreams

- A perfect time for rituals to do with prophecy and protection

- An ideal time for any work that needs additional power, such as help acquiring a new job or healing for serious conditions

WANING MOON

The waning moon, when it is growing smaller, is the ideal time to banish evil influences, decrease or remove obstacles and illness, deactivate enemies, and to remove harm. Here, "decrease" is the operative word, as the moon's light is decreasing. This is a time to cast spells to help release old, unwanted negative energies, especially those to do with addiction, illness, or depression and apathy.

CHAPTER

9

HERBS, PLANTS, FLOWERS and SPICES

Adding herbs, plants, flowers or spices to your spell increases its power and intensity, and can create the most amazing results. each has its own energy, which can be transferred to us by physical contact. You can choose to roll your candle into the herb, releasing its oils, or burn the herbs in a small fire-proof container on your altar. What follows are some examples of the herbs, plants, flowers and spices that can be used and what kind of spells they are best for.

a

acacia: protection, psychic powers, money, love

african violet: spirituality, protection

allspice: money, luck, healing

almond: money, prosperity, wisdom

aloe: protection, luck

anemone: health, protection, healing

angelica: exorcism, protection, healing, visions

apple: love, healing, garden magic, immortality

apricot: love

ash: protection, prosperity, sea rituals, health

aster: love

avocado: love, beauty

b

bamboo: protection, luck, hex-breaking, wishes

banana: fertility, potency, prosperity

basil: love, exorcism, wealth, protection when flying

bay: protection, psychic powers, healing, purification, strength

bean: protection, exorcism, wart-charming

bergamot: money, success

blackberry: healing, money, protection

bluebell: luck, truth

blueberry: protection

borage: courage, psychic powers

bracken: healing, rune magic, prophetic dreams

brazil nut: love

burdock: protection, healing

C

cabbage: luck

cactus: protection, chastity

camphor: chastity, health, divination

caper: potency, luck

caraway: protection, health, anti-theft, mental powers

cardamom: love

carnation: protection, strength, healing

carrot: fertility

cashew: money

celery: mental powers, psychic powers

chamomile: money, sleep, love, purification

chestnut: love

chicory: removing obstacles, invisibility, favours, frigidity

chilli pepper: fidelity, hex-breaking, love

chrysanthemum: protection

cinnamon: spirituality, success, healing, power

clover: protection, money, love, fidelity, exorcism, success, luck

coconut: purification, protection, chastity

coriander: love, health, healing

crocus: love, visions

cucumber: chastity, healing, fertility

cumin: protection, fidelity, exorcism

d

daffodil: love, fertility, luck

daisy: love, luck

dandelion: divination, wishes, calling spirits

dill: protection, money, luck

e

elm: love

eucalyptus: healing, protection

f

fennel: protection, healing, purification

fern: rain-making, protection, luck, riches, eternal youth, health, exorcism

fig: divination, fertility, love

foxglove: protection

g

garlic: protection, healing, exorcism, anti-theft, anti-seduction

geranium: fertility, health, love, protection

ginger: love, money, success, power

ginseng: love, wishes, healing, beauty, protection

grape: fertility, garden magic, mental powers, money

grass: psychic powers, protection

ground ivy: divination

h

hawthorn: fertility, chastity, happiness

hazel: luck, fertility, anti-lightning, protection, wishes

heather: protection, rain-making, luck

holly: protection, anti-lightning, luck, magic, balance

honesty: money, repelling monsters

honeysuckle: money, psychic powers, protection

horse chestnut: money, healing

hyacinth: love, protection, happiness

hydrangea: hex-breaking

i

iris: purification, wisdom

ivy: protection, healing

j

jasmine: love, money, prophetic dreams

juniper: protection, anti-theft, love, exorcism, health

k

knotweed: binding, health

l

lavender: love, protection, sleep, chastity

leek: love, protection, exorcism

lemon: longevity, purification, love, friendship

lemongrass: repel snakes, unwanted lust of others, psychic powers

lettuce: chastity, protection, love, divination, sleep

lilac: exorcism, protection, beauty

lily: protection, breaking love spells

lily of the valley: mental powers, happiness

lime: healing, love, protection

m

mace: psychic powers, mental powers

magnolia: fidelity

marigold: protection, prophetic dreams, business and legal matters, psychic powers

marjoram: love, happiness, health, money, healing

mimosa: love, prophetic dreams, purification

mint: money, love, luck, healing, exorcism, travel, protection

mistletoe: protection, love, hunting, fertility, health, exorcism

moss: luck, money

mustard: fertility, mental powers

n

nettle: exorcism, protection, healing

nuts: fertility, prosperity, love, luck

o

oak: protection, health, money, healing, potency, fertility, luck

oats: money

olive: healing, peace, fertility, potency

onion: protection, exorcism, healing, money

orange: love, divination, luck, money

orchid: love

p

pansy: love, rain magic, love, divination

parsley: love, protection, purification

pea: money, love

peach: love, exorcism, longevity, fertility, wishes

pear: love

pecan: money, employment

peony: financial abundance

pepper: protection, exorcism

peppermint: purification, sleep, love, healing, psychic powers

pineapple: luck, money, chastity

pistachio: breaking love spells

plum: healing

pomegranate: divination, luck, wishes, wealth, fertility

poppy: fertility, love, sleep, money, luck, invisibility

potato: image magic, healing

primrose: protection, love

q

quince: love, happiness

r

radish: protection

raspberry: love

rhubarb: protection, fidelity

rice: rain, fertility, money

rose: love, psychic powers, healing, divination, luck, protection

rosemary: protection, mental powers, exorcism, purification, healing, sleep, youth

s

saffron: love, healing, happiness

sage: immortality, longevity, wisdom, wishes

sesame: money

shallot: purification

sloe: exorcism, protection

snapdragon: brings cheerfulness

spearmint: healing, love, mental powers

star anise: psychic powers, luck

strawberry: love, luck

sunflower: fertility, wishes, health, wisdom

sweet pea: friendship, chastity, courage, strength

t

tamarind: love

tea: riches, courage, strength

thistle: strength, protection, hex-breaking, healing

thyme: health, healing, sleep, psychic powers, love, purification, courage

toadstool: rain-making

turmeric: purification, helps ease rheumatism

turnip: protection, ending relationships

V

vanilla: love, mental powers

violet: protection, luck, love, wishes, peace, healing

W

walnut: health, mental powers, infertility, wishes

Y

yellow primrose: searching for something

yucca: transmutation

CHAPTER
10

GEMS, CRYSTALS and STONES

As far as spiritual matters are concerned, the words "crystal" and "stone" are interchangeable. We aren't referring to the kind of stones that you see lying around on the beach, but the special items that you see in a New Age store that some like to call stones and others refer to as crystals. Crystals are formed in rock over a long period of time, sometimes as a result of pressure and heat. While many are pretty but not especially valuable, those that we refer to as gems or gemstones are often very valuable indeed.

Gemstones have consciousness and they are incredibly generous – able and willing to work with you for years providing you treat them accordingly. Take care to cleanse all new stones thoroughly before using them.

This can be done in several ways:

- Wash your stone under running tap water and leave it to dry on a kitchen towel
- Wash your stone in a stream or river and leave to dry in sunlight or moonlight. A full moon will add extra power

- Take your stone outside when it's raining and let the stone be washed by the rain. Let it dry naturally in sunlight or moonlight
- Some crystals will fall apart if washed, so charge them without washing them

You will then need to charge your crystal by incorporating your energy into it, so hold it in your hand, breathe on it and imagine white light coming down from the universe and filling the crystal with power. When using crystals for healing, they will pick up the energy of the disease or ailment, so you will need to cleanse and charge them again after you have finished working with them.

CRYSTALS
and GEMSTONES

Some of the following stones are not
formed in rock at all: for instance, amber
is ancient tree sap, and pearls are created
by an oyster coating an irritating piece
of grit with layers of pearl to make it
smooth. However, as far as spiritual work
is concerned, crystals, stones and gems are
useful, and none has more significance than
another, regardless of the commercial value
that may be put upon them.

agate *crystal*
  Helps by restoring energy and healing. It can
  enhance creativity and intellect, and is a good
  grounding stone. It is highly protective, and is
  often used in spells for the protection of children.

amethyst *gem*
  Provides healing on all levels – mind, body and
  spirit. It elevates vibrational frequencies and
  protects against negative energies.

amber *resin*
  Can change negative energy into positive energy.

diamond *gem*
  Increases good thoughts and feelings and
  decreases negative ones.

hematite *crystal*
  Responsible for giving perception, improves
  memory and releases anxiety, providing grounding.

lapis lazuli *crystal*
  Provides understanding and wisdom. Opens the
  third eye, leading to awareness.

moonstone *crystal*
  Creates a sense of balance.

opal *gem*

Increases emotion, perception and creativity. Very potent, but can create difficulties for the wrong person, so it needs to be used with extreme care.

pearl *created inside an oyster*

Increases purity of both mind and heart. Brings the emotions back into balance and reduces stress.

quartz *crystal*

Practical for all kinds of spellcasting.

rose quartz *crystal*

Restores harmony after emotional damage and improves any situation to do with love.

turquoise *crystal*

Highly spiritual yet grounding. Brings the chakras into alignment and opens the heart for unrestricted love.

crystals, gems, stones and star signs

Many people love to know which crystal is linked to their star sign, and opinions vary as to which is right for each sign. I have listed the various suggestions, leaving it to you to pick the ones you like best. You can choose to have an expensive gem made into a jewel or an inexpensive stone, as both are equally relevant.

star sign   crystal

star sign	crystal
Aries	Diamond, bloodstone
Taurus	Emerald, topaz, sapphire
Gemini	Agate, alexandrite, onyx
Cancer	Pearl, mother of pearl
Leo	Diamond, zircon, ruby, sardonyx, tiger's eye
Virgo	Sardonyx, diamond, chrysolite
Libra	Sapphire, emerald, jade
Scorpio	Opal, obsidian, onyx, jet, marquezite
Sagittarius	Topaz, carbuncle, sapphire
Capricorn	Turquoise, black opal, tourmaline
Aquarius	Lapis lazuli, amethyst
Pisces	Moonstone, bloodstone, pearl

CHAPTER
11

CHAKRAS

the
SEVEN
CHAKRAS

The chakras are spiritual openings that have seven centres within the body that run along the spine, starting at the base and working their way up to the top of the head. In a healthy, balanced person, the seven chakras provide the correct balance of energy to every part of the body, including the mind and spirit.

the
ROOT
CHAKRA
RED

This chakra is located at the very base of your spine, near your tailbone.

the

SACRAL CHAKRA
ORANGE

The sacral chakra is located immediately below the navel and extends to its centre.

the SOLAR PLEXUS CHAKRA

YELLOW

The solar plexus chakra starts at the centre of the navel and extends up to the breastbone.

the

HEART
CHAKRA
GREEN

The heart chakra's centre is located over your heart.

the THROAT CHAKRA

PALE BLUE

The throat chakra's centre is between the collar bones, and it radiates down to the centre of your heart and up to the centre of the eyes.

the

THIRD EYE
CHAKRA

INDIGO

The third eye chakra is in between the eyebrows.

the
CROWN
CHAKRA
VIOLET and WHITE

The crown chakra is at the crown of the head.

how to
OPEN and close the
CHAKRAS

There are several ways to open the chakras and close them down again. One method is to visualize and meditate on the colours, always starting with the base chakra. Imagine this chakra has "roots" that wend their way downwards through the earth. Then work your way upwards through each chakra in turn and imagine they are opening up like a flower bud would. All your chakras need to be open before spellcasting.

Always ensure that you close your chakras after spellcasting. This is vitally important! If you don't do this, you may find it hard to relax, or be plagued by bad dreams.

To close the chakras simply start at the top of your head and visualize the crown chakra closing, then work your way back down, chakra by chakra. When you reach the base chakra, draw up the "roots" and allow the system to settle back down.

CHAPTER

12

HERBAL SPELLCASTING

Herbal spellcasting is the skill of using herbs to cast various types of spells. It is another type of natural spellcasting, but in this case you use plants as your source of energy. Herbal spellcasting can be referred to in many ways, such as sachets, poppets, infusions, powders, ointments, oils, baths and incenses. This is a traditional form of spellcasting that can be found all over the world, under different names in most civilizations.

SACHETS

A sachet is a small bag that contains herbs. It is designed to be carried with you or placed someplace such as in your car, over a door or window, under your pillow, etc. In some cultures, a sachet may be called a "charm bag".

OILS

To make your own oil, select a vegetable oil for your base. Almond, olive, grape-seed, sunflower oil or maybe avocado oil are ideal options. Add a few drops of your chosen essential oils, pick up the container and rotate the oil clockwise while visualizing your intention for its use. You can rub it over your body or over objects to bless them. You can also rub your candles with it to strengthen their powers, and you can even let a few drops fall into your bath.

INCENSES

Incenses are made of herbs, essential oils and plant resin. In several recipes, you can even find powdered amber. For spellcasting, most incense is in a granular form, as a powder that is designed to be burned on hot charcoal in a special container.

Incense can be used in two ways: either burn it and meditate on its properties, or use it in the background while you perform other types of spellcasting.

Now that you know all the forms that refer to herbal spellcasting, here is how to cast a herbal spell. This simple method works for all types of herbal spellcasting:

Note: Before everything else, decide on the purpose of your spell and exactly what your intention is going to be.

SELECT

your herbs

Find the appropriate herbs for the purpose
of your spell. Always use good-quality
herbs as they are full of energy. This
also applies to oils, so avoid purchasing
synthetic essential oils. Organic and fresh
herbs and resins are best.

CHARGE
your herbs

Your herbs and your ingredients need to be charged. To do this, put the plants into a bowl one at a time, and rub your hands together while focusing on the plant's energy. Run your hands through the plants while still focusing on your intention. Imagine they are glowing with a beam of white or golden light.

If it is oil, just place your hands over it. Chant the plant's name, along with its properties, and burn a candle of the appropriate colour to reinforce your concentration. Stop when you feel a tingling sensation in your fingers.

When all the plants are charged, you can start using them for spells. Whichever of the methods you have chosen to use, concentrate on what you are spelling for and visualize yourself getting what you want from the spell while placing the item on your altar.

the ALTAR

Place your item on your altar and ask the appropriate Archangel to help you achieve your goal. Describe out loud what you've made and the ingredients you have used. You can also do this if you are using the bathtub method.

Keep your herbs and oils on your altar until you feel that the spell has worked. If you work with the moon phases, craft the spell at the new moon and leave it on your altar until the full moon.

When you feel that it has served its purpose or when the moon is waning, dispose of your herbal spell. Burn it, bury it or scatter the ashes to the four winds.

CHAPTER

13

HERBS,
SPICES
and
CRYSTALS

Here are the herbs and spices that will work for specific problems. You only need to use one or two of them at a time, so there are plenty to choose from. You will also see ideas for crystals that you can carry around with you for luck, and a special crystal spell to help you communicate clearly.

HEALING

Bay, Cedar, Cinnamon,
Eucalyptus, Heliotrope,
Ivy, Mugwort, Myrrh,
Nettle, Peppermint,
Pine, Rose, Rosemary,
Sandalwood,
Thyme, Vervain

LOVE

Aloes, Basil, Cardamom, Chamomile, Cinnamon, Clove, Clover, Copal, Coriander, Daisy, Dragon's Blood, Ginger, Hibiscus, Jasmine, Lavender, Peppermint, Rose, Rosemary, Thyme, Vervain, Vetiver

SEXUALITY

Cinnamon, Garlic,
Ginseng, Hibiscus,
Lemongrass, Liquorice,
Mint, Nettle, Parsley,
Patchouli, Rosemary,
Vanilla

PROSPERITY
and MONEY

Almond, Benzoin, Cedar,
Chamomile, Cinnamon,
Clove, Clover, Jasmine,
Oak, Patchouli, Pine, Tulip

PROTECTION

Acacia, Aloe, Anise, Basil, Bay, Cedar, Cinnamon, Clove, Dragon's Blood, Frankincense, Holly, Lavender, Mugwort, Myrrh, Nettle, Olive, Pine, Pepper, Rosemary, Sage, Sandalwood, Witch Hazel

PSYCHIC POWERS

Acacia, Bay, Cinnamon,
Lemongrass, Mugwort,
Peppermint, Rose, Star
Anise, Thyme

PURIFICATION

Bay, Benzoin, Cedar,
Chamomile, Copal,
Hyssop, Lavender, Parsley,
Peppermint, Rosemary,
Sage, Thyme, Vervain

CRYSTALS

Crystals can be useful in spellcasting, but they can also be used as good-luck charms that you can carry with you at all times. Choose your crystal or stone and charge it by first cleansing it and then placing it on your altar and telling it what you want it to achieve.

A good stone to consider is lapis lazuli, which is known as "a stone of truth" or "the blue stone". It links with the throat chakra for communication, so it helps to give you confidence to know what to say and when to say it. Place an amethyst or clear quartz onto your altar when charging your lapis lazuli, as this will increase the energy of the spell.

the
SPELL

- 1 piece lapis lazuli
- 1 amethyst and/or clear quartz
- 1 white or yellow candle

If you choose to use them, place the amethyst or quartz in front of the candle and light same. Hold the lapis lazuli in both hands, which will have the effect of charging it. Visualize the conversation you anticipate having, and see yourself coming out of the situation victoriously.

I call upon Archangel Gabriel to help
me with the right words to say.
To make me
victorious for another day.
So mote it be.

Keep the stone close to the amethyst or clear
quartz on your altar and leave it, together
with the candle burning, for at least one hour.

It is now ready to work with you.

OTHER CRYSTALS

You can use the same system as above,
adapting the spell to say whatever you need
it to say, and invoking whichever Archangel
meets your needs.

the
ARCHANGELS

Michael Protection, truth, integrity, strength and courage

Gabriel Communication skills, purity, harmony and creativity

Raphael Healing and travel

Uriel Solving problems and resolving conflicts, wisdom, emotional imbalance and determination

Now you can add a particular crystal to your altar to make the spell work for you. Here are some of the crystals that you might wish to use, along with their effects.

AMBER

Technically, amber isn't a crystal at all, because it is a resin, but amber is so ancient that it is solid and it acts like a crystal.

It is good to use when someone is in poor health, and an amber necklace and bracelet can be worn if you or your loved one has a cough. In olden times, women were given amber to hold or to keep in the bed with them when they were in childbirth, as it was supposed to make the process safer and easier.

ROSE
QUARTZ

This beautiful crystal is associated with romantic love and also with loving friendship.

JASPER

Jasper is a small red stone that represents two things, the first being passion and sexuality, and the second being the necessities of life, such as enough money to live on, a decent home, safety and good food to eat.

CARNELIAN

This orange crystal is associated with settled relationships, such as marriage and partnerships, but also business partnerships. It can also be useful for someone who wants to conceive. It has some link to money, in the form of abundance, or having enough on which to live comfortably.

TIGER'S EYE

This is a great crystal for times when you need confidence in yourself and when you want to prevent others from walking all over you. Once you have finished the spell, keep the tiger's eye somewhere nearby, such as a kitchen shelf or your purse.

CITRINE

This yellow stone is a form of amethyst which has been heat treated. It is not only very pretty, but it can improve a poor financial situation and give power to someone who feels powerless.

AGATE

Agate is associated with a loving heart and the ability to deal with all kinds of people fairly. It links with giving and receiving unconditional love.

BLUE LACE AGATE

A lovely crystal, blue lace agate is helpful when you are trying to get a point across or when you wish to communicate clearly. It is also good for those who are unwell. A friend of mine has "blu-tacked" a piece of blue lace agate to her computer because she swears that it keeps her computer from playing up!

SHUNGITE

While on the subject of computers, if you find yours giving you headaches and want to be able to work on it in a more relaxed way, this Russian stone will do the trick. It is also a powerful healing stone.

SODALITE

This is a healing stone which is worth keeping beside you if you are ill. It can also help you develop your intuition and your psychic powers.

AMETHYST

This stone is definitely linked to psychic ability and with the connection to the spirit world, so use it for spellcasting, but also wear a piece of amethyst as jewellery.

OBSIDIAN, HAEMATITE, MARQUEZITE

All these black stones have a protective quality, so if you are being bullied, hurt, pushed around or in any other way given a bad time by others, charge up one of these stones, use it on your altar and keep a piece of charged stone on you or nearby.

CLEAR QUARTZ

Clear quartz is less exciting to look at than any of the other crystals, but it is extremely useful because it can stand in for any crystal and you can use it for any purpose. If you only ever buy yourself one crystal, it should be a piece of clear quartz.

CHAPTER
14

SPELLS
for all
PURPOSES

Here you will find spells for many different situations or problems. Some of them have to be performed at special times, and others take time to prepare, but that helps you to focus on what needs to happen, which makes the spells more powerful.

a spell to bring
SUCCESS
in an exam, job interview or driving test

- 1 yellow candle
- 1 incense stick or essential oil, for example: lemon, lavender, jasmine, rosemary, cinnamon or peppermint
- Your study books or course material
- A pen or pencil
- A piece of paper

Light the incense and inhale and exhale three deep breaths, or until you are fully relaxed.

Take the piece of paper and draw a picture of the sun, as this links with the sun card in the Tarot, which represents passing a test. Light the yellow candle and chant the following spell:

I call upon Archangel Michael to help me pass my test,
And to help me achieve to do my best.
So mote it be.

Imagine yourself (or whatever you may be spelling for) being immersed in pure white light together with the sun's energy coming to help you and giving you strength, focus and memory when you take the exam. Visualize the sunlight radiating its light to you and clearing your mind so you can pass the exam. Keep the drawing with you, as it will act as your lucky charm during the test.

I call upon Archangel Michael
to give me the confidence I need.
Strength too is what I require.
I ask that you grant me my heart's
desire.
So mote it be.

Let the candle burn right down.

This spell can boost confidence, give strength
and make you more appealing to others,
depending on your needs.

a

CONFIDENCE

spell

• 1 white candle

Sit, relax and meditate while concentrating
on your intention as to what you are
spellcasting for.

Light the white candle on your altar.

a spell to REMOVE a CURSE

In order to eliminate bad luck, it is necessary to do a double-intention good-luck spell. However, one of the simplest ways is to take a salt bath to wash away any negativity that may be clinging to you and to light a green candle. While bathing, imagine the negativity being washed away and replaced with positivity. Cinnamon also has cleansing properties that eliminate unacceptable energies and invite good luck.

- 1 green candle
- Cinnamon powder
- Salt

Place the green candle on your altar and pour
salt around it, thereby making a protective circle.
Light the candle.

I call upon Archangel Michael to remove
all and any bad luck from me.
Replace this with good luck and lots
of positivity.
So mote it be.

Concentrate, focus and imagine all the problems
in your life disappearing.

After ten minutes, shake the cinnamon powder
over the salt. Imagine a pure white light
descending over you while you think about all
the good things you want in your life.
Let the candle burn right down.

Place the banknote inside the chest or box.
Place a garlic head on top of the money.

I call upon Archangel Uriel to
bring me money.
Enough for my needs to make
my life sunny.
So mote it be.

Now place the basil leaves on top of the
money. Pour several drops of the oil of your
choice onto a white handkerchief, then place
this on top of the basil leaves. Close the chest
or box and put it under your bed. Leave it
undisturbed for twenty-eight days and do not
tell anyone about it.

a spell to
ATTRACT
MONEY

Basil is a good strong herb to use in order to attract money to you.

- A wooden chest (or any box)
- 1 banknote of a high denomination
- 1 garlic head
- 5 fresh basil leaves
- Essential oil, such as bergamot, cinnamon, myrrh, sandalwood or ginger
- A white handkerchief

a spell to keep and
PROTECT
your job

This spell can help you keep and protect your job as well as protecting yourself from negativity. It is an easy spell that will transfer the energy of the full moon to your clothes or home by simply chanting. This is a good way to channel positive intentions and the best way to capture lunar energy is by preparing "Full Moon Water" during the previous full moon.

- 1 bowl of Full Moon Water

To make your Full Moon Water, fill a small container and leave it outside overnight in the light of a full moon to absorb the moon's energy.

Be sure to prepare your Full Moon Water during the previous full moon at night. Lay out on your bed the clothes that you intend to wear to work that day. Sprinkle some Full Moon Water on them and say:

I call upon Archangel Michael to give me protection both in my work and personal life,
And ask that you replace all negativity with plenty of affection.
So mote it be.

Picture all the good things that will happen while chanting. If you wish, this can be used as a daily ritual to begin your day with confidence. You can also use this spell if you are feeling under stress as it will lighten your mood and will help to keep you grounded. You can change the spell to fit your requirements, or to keep you protected from any negativity in your workplace, at home, at school or college.

175

Insert the cinnamon incense stick into the wooden incense holder and light it. Chant the following as many times as you wish:

I call upon Archangel Michael to remove from me the negativity that seems to have stuck,
And bring me instead prosperity and luck.
So mote it be.

As the incense burns, visualize its purifying properties purging every corner of your house and protecting you from negative influences.

a spell for
GOOD LUCK
and PROSPERITY

Wood is naturally charged with the undeniable positive vibrations of trees. Cinnamon is a psychic cleanser that can be used to purify the home and body from negative influences. Burning cinnamon will send a precise message that attracts friendly spirits. Improvement in the energies in your home, personal spaces or workplace can be achieved with this spell.

- Cinnamon incense
- Wooden incense holder

CHAPTER

15

MAKING SPELLS WORK

TIPS

and HINTS

You may wonder why
your spells don't work,
and there may be several
reasons, but the tips
on the following pages
should help.

1. You need to eliminate all doubts and uncertainty within yourself.
2. Never tell anyone about the spell you have been working on.
3. Choose the correct colours, symbols and ingredients relevant to your spell.
4. When you invite in your Archangel, make sure you understand why.
5. It is important to practise meditation and visualizations so they become second nature.
6. Familiarize yourself with the current moon phase.
7. Most importantly: have faith in yourself, because the power comes from within.

additional
TIPS

1. Before spellcasting, understand how and why the spell works.

2. Casting spells that are successful for you is really a voyage of self-discovery.

3. You will only realize what works for you after conducting numerous spells.

4. Never give up.

5. If on your first attempt, your spell did not produce the effect you wanted, try again; perhaps with different things on your altar. Try different techniques, but change the way you do the spell rather than repeating the same one.

casting a
CIRCLE
of
PROTECTION

Although not absolutely necessary, it is a
good idea to conduct your spellcasting
within a circle of protection. You can do
this by lighting a sage stick and waving it
over yourself and your altar.

TAKE YOURSELF

into consideration

1. Do not conduct any spellcasting on a full stomach.
2. On the day you wish to begin a spell, it is best to avoid drinking alcohol, and keep away from all drugs except for any that have been medically prescribed.

3. Take good care of your body and be in a good physical condition.

4. Exercise is an excellent way of grounding yourself. Walking, dancing or even practicing yoga are all good options to choose from.

5. Relax. You should never cast a spell if you are feeling physically exhausted, as spellcasting can use a lot of your energy.

6. Do not continue with your spellcasting if you are feeling pain of any kind, feeling fearful or are experiencing any form of depression.

VISUALIZATION

Some of the most powerful spells can be achieved purely through visualization, so it is important that you practise this skill. This is achieved by concentrating your mind on a specific object or wish and imagining what it looks and feels like.

If you are not a visual person, but rather an auditory person, try listening to music, sounds or singing mantras.

Think of a song that will place you in the correct mindset for what you are trying to create. For example, if you're working on a love spell, sing "All You Need Is Love".

If you are a sensory person, look for materials that you can touch, such as clothes, sand, stones, feathers or whatever may stimulate your consciousness and will make you become more aware of your existence. For example, if you are spellcasting for money, hold a coin or a note in your hand, feel its texture, and connect with its energy and vibration.

CONFIDENCE, PATIENCE and UNDERSTANDING

- It is important that you believe that the spell will work,

- Never spell just to see if it works or for entertainment,

- Never talk about a spell that you are working on. No one else needs to know about your spellcasting,

- As we all have, you will learn by making mistakes as you slowly gain experience, but with patience and determination, you will find what works for you,

- You have no doubt heard of the expression "everything in its own time". This also applies to everything in the universe. Therefore, it is necessary to be patient. When the time is right, it will and does happen. This can also apply to your spellcasting.

- Once you have performed your spellcasting, you must relax and await the outcome patiently.

- Any apprehension will only get in the way of the result you desire.

- If a spell has not worked for you or brought you the expected results, understand that the timing is not right for you.

- Take time out in order to refocus and look at different ways of how you can spell from a new viewpoint.

- Do not be afraid to experiment with different techniques until you find what suits you best.

- You can make your spells more powerful by being creative, such as by writing your own spells and putting your own intentions into them.

- Experiment with different objects, crystals, colours, herbs etc.

- You will learn something new with each spell, and this is perfectly normal.

CONCLUSION

never cast spells to cause harm to others, because the harm will come back on you three times as badly.

always remember to keep an eye on candles while they are burning and never to leave them unguarded.

remember to follow the guidelines and always to work for the good of all concerned. Do not be afraid to experiment with all the different materials that are available to you and remember to be patient and not to expect immediate results. As with everything, spellcasting takes practice, practice and more practice! Good luck!